Magic Squares and More

Written by Claire Owen

China

My name is Lin. I live in China, which is the home of many important inventions and ideas. How do you think mathematics was used in ancient China?

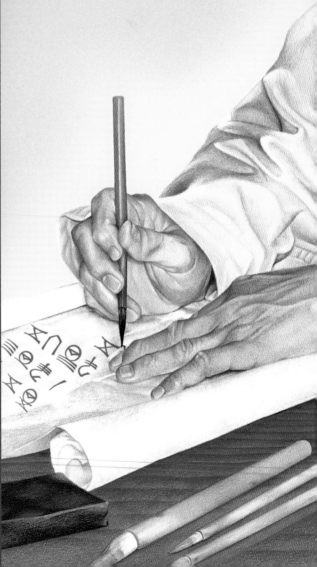

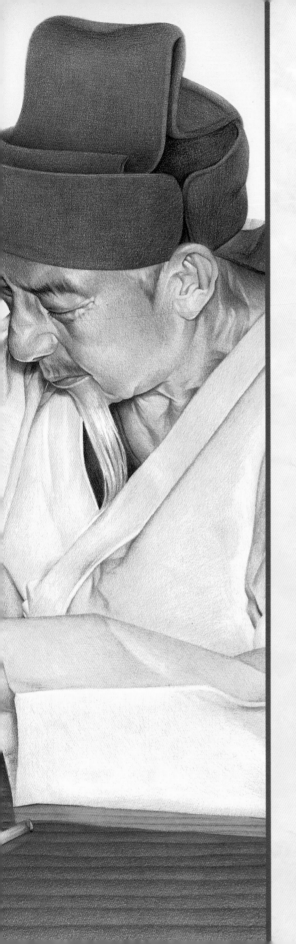

Contents

Wherever you see me, you'll find activities to try and questions to answer.

Made in China

The Chinese have made many important scientific inventions and mathematical discoveries over the last 2,000 years. However, the use of mathematics in China can be traced back even further. The earliest examples of Chinese numerals were found on "dragon bones" that are 4,000 years old!

Earthquake detectors (left) were first made in China in the year 132. When an earthquake occurs, a ball drops from a dragon's mouth into a frog's mouth! This shows the direction of the earthquake.

numeral a symbol that represents a number

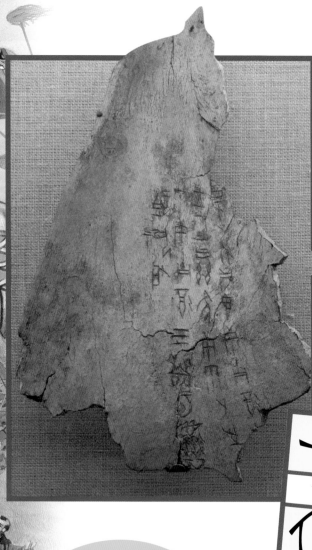

"Dragon bones" are actually ox bones and tortoise shells (left). Some Chinese believed they could use dragon bones to tell the future.

Some ancient Chinese numerals are shown on the chart below.

What numbers are these?

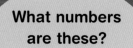

Draw the Chinese numeral for 1,234.

1	2	3	4	5
6	7	8	9	10
20	30	40	50	60
100	200	300	400	500
1,000	2,000	3,000	4,000	5,000

The First Magic Square

The earliest example of a magic square comes from China. According to an ancient Chinese legend, the emperor saw a turtle in the Lo River. On the turtle's back were groups of dots that showed numbers. After the emperor figured out the secret of the numbers, he called the magic square "Lo Shu."

Lo Shu Magic Square

Can you figure out what is "magic" about the Lo Shu square? (Hint: Add the three numbers in any row, column, or diagonal, as shown below.)

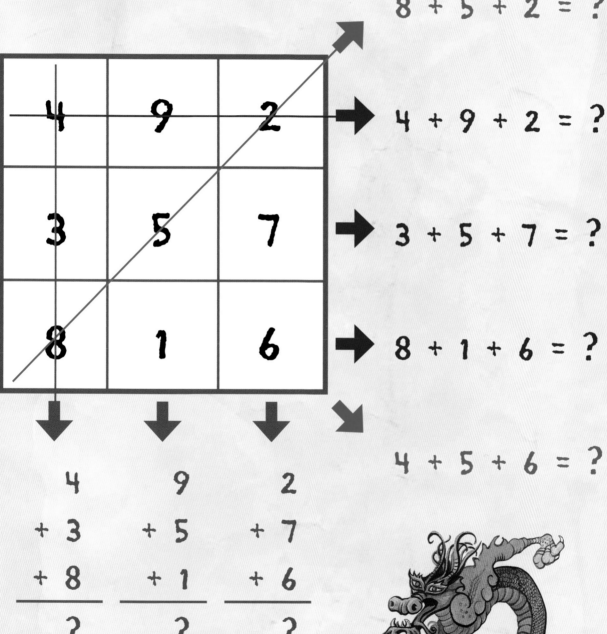

$$8 + 5 + 2 = ?$$

$$4 + 9 + 2 = ?$$

$$3 + 5 + 7 = ?$$

$$8 + 1 + 6 = ?$$

$$4 + 5 + 6 = ?$$

$$\begin{array}{r} 4 \\ + 3 \\ + 8 \\ \hline ? \end{array} \qquad \begin{array}{r} 9 \\ + 5 \\ + 1 \\ \hline ? \end{array} \qquad \begin{array}{r} 2 \\ + 7 \\ + 6 \\ \hline ? \end{array}$$

More Magic Squares

The Lo Shu magic square shows the numbers 1 through 9. It is called a three-by-three (3 x 3) magic square because it has three rows and three columns. Almost 900 different four-by-four magic squares can be made from the numbers 1 through 16! However, the numbers in a magic square do not have to start from 1.

A

10	15	14
17	13	9
12	11	?

B

4	14	12
18	?	2
8	6	16

C

2	7	11	14
16	9	5	4
13	12	8	1
3	6	?	15

For each of these incomplete magic squares, figure out the "magic" total of each row, column, or diagonal. Then find the missing number.

Make a Magic Square

You will need plain paper or grid paper.

1. Use blue to draw a grid for a 3 x 3 magic square. Then use red to add 4 more boxes.

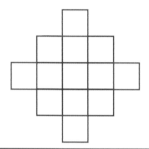

2. Pick any starting number (for example, 20). Write it in the red square at the left.

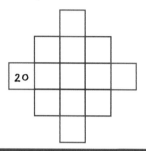

3. Write the next 8 numbers in the order shown by this example.

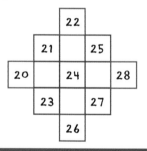

4. Cross out the starting number. Write it inside the blue square, on the far side.

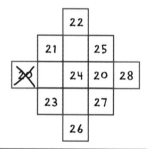

5. Do the same thing for each of the other numbers in red boxes.

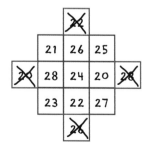

6. To check that you have made a magic square, add the numbers in each row, column, or diagonal.

21	26	25
28	24	20
23	22	27

Pointing the Way

The world's first compass was invented in China about 2,000 years ago. The "pointer" was a ladle carved from lodestone. When the ladle was balanced on a circle of polished bronze, the handle pointed to the south. Compasses like this were used to help decide where a house should be built or how a city should be laid out.

lodestone   magnetic iron ore

Follow the Compass

1. On the "map" below, start at the ⬭ near
   the birds. Go 7 squares west. Then go 8 squares south.
   Where did you finish?

2. Pick two pictures on the "map." Write directions
   for moving from one picture to the other.
   Ask a partner to follow your directions.

The Chinese Abacus

The *suan-pan*, or Chinese abacus, was invented about 800 years ago. Using "columns" of beads in a frame, it is possible to do sums very quickly. The abacus is still used in Asia today, although many young people prefer to use an electronic calculator.

electronic   controlled by electrical parts, such as microchips

Children in China are taught how to use an abacus at school.

Did You Know?

In ancient Rome, counting boards were drawn in the dust. The word *abacus* comes from the Greek word *abax*, which means a table covered with dust. The word *calculate* comes from the pebbles that were used on the counting board. These pebbles were called *calculi* in Latin.

Reading the Beads

Starting from the right, the "columns" of a
Chinese abacus show ones, tens, hundreds,
and so on. To show a number, beads are pushed
up or down to the crossbar.* Each bead below
the crossbar shows one. Each bead above the
crossbar shows five. The picture below shows
the number 1,527.

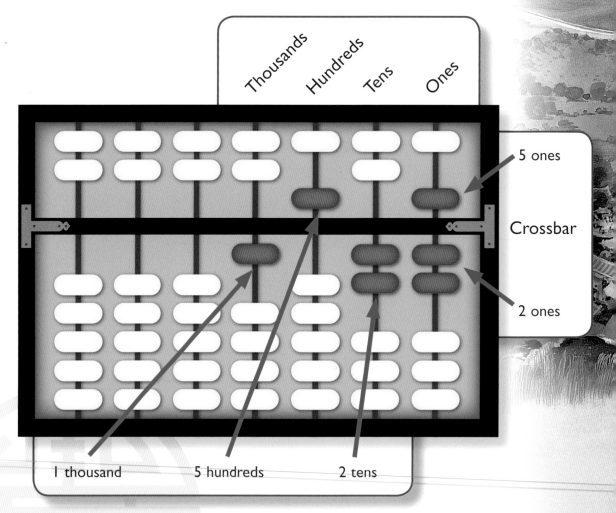

* On this page, those beads have been shown in red.

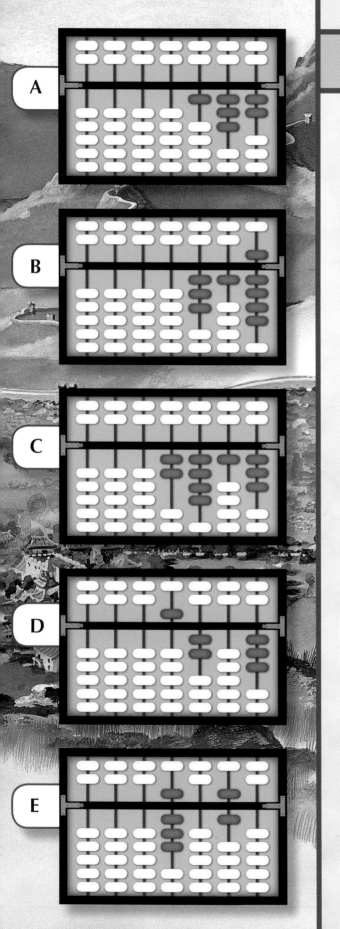

A

B

C

D

E

1. Which abacus (A to E) shows the number 5,203?

2. What numbers do the other abacus pictures show?

3. Pretend that you are going to show the number 4,216 on this abacus.

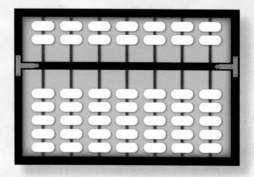

How many beads would you need to move to the crossbar?

4. James used the abacus above. He moved three beads to the crossbar. He made a number less than 10,000.

   a. What is the smallest number James could have made?

   b. What is the greatest number James could have made?

   c. List some other numbers that James could have made.

Sample Answers

Page 5   2,325

             3,104

Page 7   The total of each row, column, or diagonal is 15.

Page 8   A: 39, 16   B: 30, 10   C: 34, 10

Page 11   1. at the bridge

Page 15   1. D

             2. A: 132   B: 319
                 C: 2,413   E: 8,060

             3. 9 beads

             4. a. 3   b. 7,000

You might like to find out about some other things that were invented in China. These include paper, porcelain, fireworks, and the umbrella!

Index